LONDON`S 100-YEAR

Photographer: Danial Emani
Design and Edit: Jevgenija Bitt
Text: Charlie Coombes

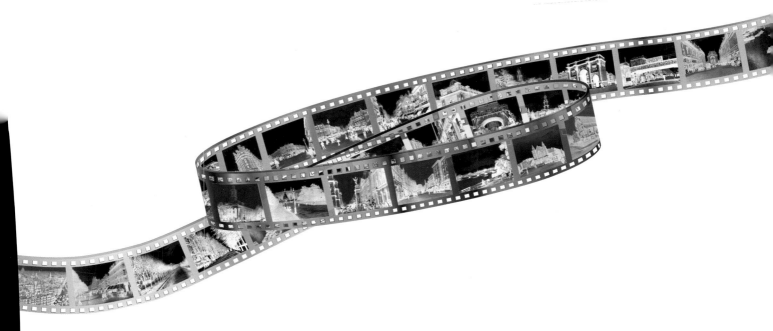

THIS BOOK WAS
SELF-PUBLISHED IN 2018
BY

DANIAL EMANI

ISBN
978-1-9164277-0-9

WWW.DANIAL.UK
WWW.MOMENTOFLIFE.COM

CONTENTS

ABOUT THE AUTHOR

Danial Emani`s London journey began in 2012, as a driver, which allowed him to find his way and discover his passion for life. London's alluring beauty persuaded Danial to purchase his first camera. Back then, he simply wanted to learn something new and capture the beauty and magic of London life. He also hoped that photography would help him to be more focused, conscious and present. As a child, Danial suffered from attention deficit disorder, often making him hyperactive and unable to concentrate; however, this did not diminish his curiosity and desire to solve as many of the world's mysteries as he could.

Danial spent two years taking photographs for pleasure and was fortunate enough to take some beautiful images of London, leading him to attempt to sell them in popular tourist markets such as Camden, Portobello and Smithfield in 2014. He was overcome by the wonderful and supportive feedback that he received from visitors. Danial returned to his driving job even more focussed on and passionate about photography, than he had been about anything else in his life.

Danial started building up his professional portfolio and continued to develop new and innovative ideas about photography. This is when the idea for 'London's 100-Year Journey' was spawned, starting with just five locations, printed on canvas, and has now grown to more than 50 and has morphed into a book.

INTRODUCTION

Since 2012, I have driven 250,000 miles during the course of my driving job and have taken more than 50,000 photographs. Many of these photos became a part of my 'London's 100-Year Journey' photo book project. As the project began to take shape, I started to perform research and realised the scale of the project that I had undertaken. Once I had found enough old photos of London, I started the long and thoroughly enjoyable process of exploring each place: wandering through those beautiful streets, comparing the different architectural styles and finding the right angle, became a work of art in itself. A magical hunt, through one of the most incredible cities in the world.

I was inspired by how much London had changed and how it seemed to be in a constant state of evolution and flux. How the people that lived in each place came to define its characteristics and how great it is to live each moment. For me, London is a metaphor for humanity and how the march of technology and progress continues, unabated. Jean Paul Sartre believed that humanity.

Looking at pictures from 100 years ago, I could not help but think that the people in them had no idea how life would be in the future, just as it is impossible for us to imagine what the next 100 years have in store and what impact, if any, our actions will have on the generations that come after us.

Danial Emani, 2018

Birds View

These two views from the highest point of the Monument perfectly encapsulate the great paradigm shift that has taken place in London's thinking, direction and culture.

One hundred years ago at the height of Britain's Imperial glory, faithful Londoners built monument steeples puncturing the air, whereas modern London has a new faith: The Church of Capitalism, where cranes stand above gigantic new structures.

The Mall

The Mall represents one of the most important ceremonial locations in England and plays a vital role
in the State Opening of Parliament, the Trooping of the Colour
and the Changing of the Guards.

The latter can be seen occurring in both pictures: a testament to Britain's almost unique ability to cling on to archaic traditions. It is also slightly ironic to see that in the present, mounted police are now required to protect soldiers from harm. It has always been an English tradition that the police are unarmed.

Fleet Street

Trafalgar Square

Trafalgar Square

Trafalgar Square is one of central London's largest open areas, making it highly suitable for large-scale protests and public celebrations; you name it, and Trafalgar has seen them all.

The two pictures show Britain's glorious National Gallery on the left containing works by Holbein, Titian, Caravaggio, Turner and many, many more. Its mock Athenian architecture reminds us of the affinity that the British felt with Athens.

Griffin Statue

The glorious Griffin Statue marks the official entrance to the City of London. The City is London's historical heart and is the place where the original Roman town was built over two millennia ago.

The City of London Corporation governs the square mile based on their own interests,
with the Griffin (which is actually a dragon) being their symbol.

Victoria Embankment

King's Cross Station

King's Cross has always been a transport hub, connecting London to the rest of the country and in recent years this has become even truer, with its sister station St Pancras now connecting London to Europe.

It is therefore a vibrant area that throbs with life, as busy people go about their busy days. This can be seen in both pictures as the cars, horse carriages and people move around the busy station, similar to ants around a nest.

Bank of England

Buckingham Palace

Buckingham Palace has been the official London residence of the monarch since Queen Victoria came to the throne in 1837.

Buckingham Palace is one of the most famous landmarks in the world. The difference between past and present is fascinating and represents the changing face of the monarchy. One hundred years ago, many countries had powerful monarchies, meaning that nobody needed to come to visit: a monarch was simply a fact of life, while today it is unique to Britain.

Sloane Street

Bond Street has always been synonymous with luxury and extravagance: its stunning Georgian houses and expensive shops offer a variety of products to the very highest echelons of London's society.

The two pictures both capture this street in their own unique way. As the world of fashion, luxury and excess moves on, so too do the purveyors of it and most of the shops of 100 years ago will have withered a long time ago, making it interesting that Fenwick's has lasted so long.

Marble Arch

Chelsea Embankment

At first glance, Chelsea Embankment appears to be an anomaly: suspended in time, while the rest of the world changes around it.

Few, if any, other places in London would be brazen enough to so completely ignore the ravages of time. With the same houses, overlooking the same trees and the same retro lampposts tucked away on the bridge behind them; even the pavement looks unchanged. Yet, even in this apparent time warp, the more careful observer can see a few signs of modernity: on the right-hand side of the road, every other tree has been replaced by a lamppost, while the horse-drawn carriages have been replaced by an array of fancy vehicles. Chelsea has always been one of the wealthiest parts of London and perhaps that is what the photograph tells us.

Oxford Circus

Charing Cross

The official center of London, despite not actually being its geographical centre, Charing Cross is the place where all distances to other places are measured from. In both the present and the past, it is London's heart: throbbing with people as they go about their busy days.

It is also interesting to use the historical center to reflect on how big the city was and still is: in 1800, the population was approximately one million. By 1900, this had grown to 6.5 million and in the present day it is around 10.5 million.

St. Thomas' Hospital

Regent Street

Named after the Prince Regent in 1810, much of Regent Street is still owned by the Crown Estate. Almost every building on the street is also listed, meaning that it is essentially impossible for them to change in any significant way.

Which explains why the buildings in the two photographs are so similar; however, the fact that they are architecturally stunning may also have something to do with it.

Regent Street

Smithfield Market

Smithfield, one of the oldest and largest meat markets in the world, has always played a crucial role in London's life.

The large-roofed building refurbished by the City of London Corporation in the late 19th century is a hive of activity: with butchers, farmers and a whole host of others enthusiastically trading. The pictures draw out the logistical change that has occurred over the past century.

45

Madame Tussauds

Seven Sisters

Seven Sisters has always been home to the city's many immigrant communities. The contrast between the two pictures brings this out wonderfully: rich areas tend to hold on to their history, whilst poorer areas are forced to move with the times.

The quiet residential area of 100 years ago is far busier, packed with shops and traffic:
the quiet places to sit are no more and everything is louder.

Whitehall

Tower of London

The Tower of London is a metaphor for how London has changed over the past 100 years, a symbol of power for many generations (while also moonlighting as a famous prison, a zoo and the centre of the government's power.

Times have changed and now it is no longer a prison: Londoners have rehabilitated the Tower and hold a special place for it in their hearts.

Kingsway

St. Mary`s Church

Lest We Forget

For more than 600 years, a Christian church stood on the Whitechapel road. During the so-called Blitz, on 29th December 1940, an enemy fire raid destroyed the church. It was left in disrepair until it was finally demolished in 1952.

Elizabeth Tower/Westminster

A view of Parliament and Big Ben down London's throbbing artery, the Thames, Victoria Embankment is a beautiful place, which is now a busy tourist hotspot: it is the perfect place to take in many of London's spectacular sights.

In the picture of 100 years ago, the city is shrouded in smog, a by-product of London's coal-burning industrialisation. There is no visible pollution in the picture above. However, modern pollution is invisible. Let`s hope that the people of the future can enjoy a London where the air is fresh.

Victoria Street

Westminster Bridge

The Mother of Parliaments in all her neo-gothic splendour: this is probably
the defining image of London for every generation.

Thankfully, very little has changed: Big Ben still stands, and democracy still lives in Britain. It may seem like the bedrock of our entire social structure, but it is really a modern construct: for instance, women still could not vote at the time of the first photograph.

Brixton Road

Geraldine Street

The spread of the car is clear for all to see and almost every person on the street owns one these days, although whether that is strictly necessary in a place such as London, where public transport is good, is another matter. However, the largest contrast between the two pictures involves the people: in the past you can get a sense of community.

A quiet leafy suburban street, Geraldine street is the kind of place that Londoners love to live in.

Greenwich Park

This park provides a profound demonstration of just how huge London has become: the contrast between the past and the present is stark. The National Maritime Museum is the largest object on view in the past, with perhaps a few chimney stacks rising behind it.In contrast, in the present, it is completely dwarfed by the giants that have been built behind it.

The picture is taken from the spot where time itself is measured, a place where Britain's greatest astronomers spent many long hours expanding human knowledge.

Church of Sacred Heart

Waterloo Palace

The first picture shows the memorial to the Crimean War, while the second has had the feminine hero of the war added to it: Florence Nightingale, a nurse who revolutionised the treatment of wounded soldiers during the conflict. It puts into context just how far society has come in terms of gender politics over the past 100 years, during which time women were given the vote in 1928.

Let us hope that the people of the future live in a society where the quality of one's actions, rather than the circumstances of one's birth, is the only thing that matters.

Pembridge Road

Green Park

The saplings have grown into mighty trees and Green Park now lives up to its name. Victoria's monument, so prominent 100 years ago, has been obscured by the autumnal beauty of London's nature.

**What kind of world will we leave to the Londoners of 100 years' time,
will we dare to protect our nature?**

Westbourne Grove

Notting Hill Gate

Notting Hill Gate has changed significantly over the years, having originally been a chaotic and disorganised street, full of boutique shops and houses.

However, in the 1950s, it had to sacrifice itself to keep the cooler and more cultural Portobello Road the same, being widened to allow more traffic through it. The results of this change can be clearly seen, as cars pour through the busy road in the present-day picture.

Hyde Park

Kensington Park Road

The minimal contrast between the two pictures obscures the radical changes that have come across the area in the past 100 years. Kensington park road and the surrounding areas have always been a busy and metropolitan area, which is perfectly illustrated by the bustling Londoners who are keen to get on with their busy days.

However, perhaps the starkest and most powerful image is the man crossing the road with a Zimmer frame, which was unthinkable 100 years ago; our society is increasingly used to people having long lives.

St. Pauls view from Thames

Tower Bridge

Tower Bridge is an undying image of London, architecturally stunning and mechanically brilliant.

When it was built in 1892, it was the most sophisticated bridge in the world, rising up 86 degrees, to let boats through.

Hammersmith Bridge

Chiswick

View from Richmond Bridge

Humans are attracted to water and something inside of us, be it genetic or cultural, drives us towards living close to it. London is lucky enough to have many different sources of water: the most famous of which is of course the Thames. However, Richmond is just as idyllic: providing a serene place for Londoners to escape from the hustle and bustle of the busy city.

The two pictures perfectly draw this out and the lack of change over 100 years is so incredible that one could imagine that they were taken on the same day. It is almost as if the same boats are for hire: offering the chance to satiate that seemingly most basic of human instincts.

Thayer Street

Ladbroke Grove

Ladbroke Grove, past and present, represents much of what has changed in London over the years. The past is filled with the markers of industry, with what appears to be a whiskey factory standing in the background and a butcher having his shoes shined in the middle of the street.

The station itself seems largely unchanged, although the great western line signs have of course been replaced by ones indicating the London Underground. But by far the starkest image in either picture is the carefully camouflaged CCTV camera: reminding us of how different the times are. Londoners lived differently back then and no human can hold back the river of time.

Regents Park

Hampstead High Street

Hampstead has always been an affluent part of London and has been home to many famous artists throughout its history: Keats, Freud, D.H. Lawrence, Constable and Galsworthy. Both pictures demonstrate a vibrant culture of shops and pubs. Not much has changed on the street and it remains narrow and busy, although if you look into the distance, one can see that the clock tower has lost its steeple.

Will Hampstead still be home to creative people in 100 years' time, or will the explosion of London's house prices mean that artists can no longer afford to call anywhere in the city, home?

105

Covent Garden

Maida Vale Canal

London's many canals stand as a monument to poor planning: originally designed to be at the very heart of London's infrastructure, they were quickly overtaken by the railway as a method to transport goods. The two pictures are the perfect representation of this state: the orderly trees and well-kept banks of 100 years ago have been replaced by the chaos of nature today.

**The many pleasure and house boats demonstrate the resourcefulness of Londoners: no place can be wasted.
The question therefore arises: What kind of infrastructure legacy will we leave the next generation?**

St Pauls

St Paul's Cathedral is the most symbolic building in London and its steeple was the highest point in the city for over 1,400 years. That finally ceased to be the case in 1967, and it is now dwarfed by the giants that surround it. It is incredible to think that in just 100 years, the tallest building in London has gone from St Paul's at 111 m to the Shard, which stands at an impressive 310 m. How far will this phenomenon go? Will we builder higher and higher, as the battle for space amongst London's most desirable areas roars on?

'No man ever steps in the same river twice,
for it's not the same river and he's not the same man'

–

HERACLITUS

The great Greek Philosopher Heraclitus argued that it would be impossible to step in the same river twice, because as soon as one stepped out of the river, the water would flow down it and by the time one got back in, you would be standing in a different river. The same is true of cities: the beautiful, amazing and incredible thing about them is that they are forever changing, transforming and becoming something new. This is the idea that I wanted to draw out during this project, showing the difference between the London of 100 years ago and today. I aim to use that as a springboard to gaze into London's ever-changing future.

Heraclitus may have said it about rivers two-and-a-half-thousand years ago, but my motto is:

'No man ever steps into the same London twice, for it's not the
same London and he's not the same man'

–

DANIAL EMANI, 2018